We dedicate this book to all curious and creative children who find joy in colors and strokes. May this book be a world of adventures and discoveries, where your imagination can fly freely and paint the most vibrant dreams. May each page be an invitation to explore, create, and enchant. May the magic of colors accompany them on all journeys, making their lives happier.

Família JTT
2024

This Book Belongs to:

○──────────────────────────────○

F.J.P.©
family's jtt publications

Test Color Page